AF378984

A New Resonance

11

Emerging Voices in
English-Language Haiku

Edited by Jim Kacian & Julie Warther

A New Resonance 11:
Emerging Voices in English-Language Haiku

© 2019 by Jim Kacian
for Red Moon Press
All Rights Reserved

Second Printing

Published by
Red Moon Press
PO Box 2461
Winchester VA
22604-1661 USA
www.redmoonpress.com

ISBN 978-1-947271-38-8

All work published with permission of the individual
authors or their accredited agents.

Cover Painting: *The Little Bridge, Pontoise* (1875)
by Camille Pisarro.
Oil canvas, 81.5 x 65.5 cm.
Kunsthalle Mannheim (Mannheim, Germany(.
Public domain.

Foreword

Entering it third decade as a part of the haiku calendar, the New Resonance project faces the inevitable changes that any long-term program must. Most signficantly, we say goodbye and thanks to Dee Evetts, who served as co-editor to the project since its inception in 1999. His deep knowledge of the genre and impeccable taste have marked each of the first 10 volumes of this series, and it has been a pleasure to work closely with him in realizing our vision of what it might become.

Moving forward, we are greatly pleased to welcome Julie Warther aboard as new co-editor. Julie is already well-known throughout the haiku world, not only for her finely crafted poems, but also as a judge of keen appreciation, and an indefatiguable organizer and promoter of the genre. What is most satisfying to us, however, is that she is a member of the New Resonance community herself, and so the process has come full circle, inspiring engagement on the one hand, and then inclusion on the other. We hope this is self-repeating, and if it is, we can anticipate that New Resonance will remain in good hands and as part of the haiku calendar well into the future.

The gathering of poets in this current volume is remarkable in many ways, and we feel you will be challenged, amused, outraged and mollified at turns, but in the end will be certain of the health of the genre as it resides in the hands of its new voices. We wish you good reading.

Jim Kacian & Julie Warther
Series Editors

A New Resonance

11

Debbi Antebi

Joseph Salvatore Aversano

Paul Chambers

Terri L French

Joshua Gage

Brent Goodman

Tia Haynes

Jessica Latham

Anna Maris

Elliot Nicely

Jacquie Pearce

Sandi Pray

Sharon Pretti

Dave Read

Hansha Teki

Angela Terry

Lew Watts

Debbi Antebi

Educational Consultant

Born June 1983
Istanbul Turkey
Currently resides
London United Kingdom

The human condition is marked with feelings of dissatisfaction. We repeatedly find ourselves spurred to try something new, only to struggle to maintain that change then finally slip back and start all over again. Antebi explores this cycle with honesty and hope, evidenced in such phrases as "unknotting", "no use hiding" and "letting my guard down". There is a vulnerability too in these poems — moonflowers are open, a painting is painted over, a photo album shows blank pages — that in fact is a requirement of striving toward newness. At times Antebi's poems tease the edges of personification — we see light that paints, rain clouds that cry and a moon that starts over. In this we discover our own humanness, and a way to navigate through difficulty and gather sweetness, even if the best we might hope for is to "stay the same".

Credits

how easily　　*Blithe Spirit 28.1*
morning light　　*Modern Haiku 49.1*
unknotting　　*Creatrix 41*
waterfall　　*brass bell*
daylilies　　*Akitsu Quarterly*
low tide　　*Prune Juice 22*
cut flowers　　*tinywords 17.2*
rain clouds　　*haikuniverse*
moonflowers　　*Inner Voices*
after rain　　*Presence 60*
learning to eat　　*The Heron's Nest XX.1*
thumbing through　　*Frogpond 41.3*
snow moon　　*Otata 12*
new home　　*failed haiku 1.6*
all those changes　　*Sonic Boom 10*

"unknotting" won the Creatrix Haiku First Prize (2018); "cut flowers" was shortlisted for The Touchstone Awards for Individual Poems (The Haiku Foundation, 2017); "learning to eat" won *The Heron's Nest* Award and the Grand Prize in The Readers' Choice Awards (2018); it also previously appeared in *a hole in the light: The Red Moon Anthology 2018* (Red Moon Press, 2019), as did "all those changes"; "thumbing through" will appear in *All the Way Home: Aging in Haiku Anthology* (Middle Island Press, 2019); "new home" was shortlisted for The Touchstone Awards for Individual Poems (The Haiku Foundation, 2016).

how easily you start over new moon

morning light
painting over
my painting

unknotting
the phone cord
mother's day

waterfall mist
the words at the tip
of my tongue

daylilies letting my guard down

low tide
no use hiding
my flaws

cut flowers
the short life
of compliments

daylilies letting my guard down

rain clouds
carrying the weight
of a grudge

moonflowers
mother opens up
about her dreams

after rain
the silence
of leaves

learning to eat
around bruises
winter apples

thumbing through
an old rolodex
winter light

snow moon
blank spaces
in a family album

new home
we unpack
our old habits

all those changes to stay the same bonsai

Debbi Antebi

Joseph Salvatore Aversano

Paul Chambers

Terri L French

Joshua Gage

Brent Goodman

Tia Haynes

Jessica Latham

Anna Maris

Elliot Nicely

Jacquie Pearce

Sandi Pray

Sharon Pretti

Dave Read

Hansha Teki

Angela Terry

Lew Watts

Joseph Salvatore Aversano

English Teacher

Born 12 December 1973
Brooklyn NY
Currently resides
Izmir (Smyrna) Turkey

Aversano writes some of the most elusive haiku to be found today, reminiscent of the early work of Martin Shea. What is elusive is not their content — here you will find birds and moons, wind and the sea, familiar material in the annals of haiku. What is rare, and rarified, in this work are the comparisons. He will link that sea with all the senses; he will join that wind to every part of us. We might call such arrangements of words "scent links", which can be difficult to pull off consistently — they require a sure ear and much patience. The poet is quite good at them, and so we become accustomed to the indirect way we are asked to maneuver within each to find its home truth. Our efforts thereafter are amply rewarded, as we come to know what a sufficient "quotient of blue" might be, or what a prayer, in the end, might aspire to.

Credits

<table>
<tr><td align="right">calling</td><td>A Hundred Gourds 5.2</td></tr>
<tr><td align="right">silence</td><td>Frogpond 36.3</td></tr>
<tr><td align="right">wind the sound</td><td>moongarlic e-Zine 2</td></tr>
<tr><td align="right">all of the senses</td><td>Akitsu Quarterly Summer 2018</td></tr>
<tr><td align="right">god</td><td>otata 15</td></tr>
<tr><td align="right">the call to prayer</td><td>Modern Haiku 49.3</td></tr>
<tr><td align="right">a bird note</td><td>otata 10</td></tr>
<tr><td align="right">it's enough</td><td>Sonic Boom 12</td></tr>
<tr><td align="right">the poplar's way</td><td>Otoliths 38</td></tr>
<tr><td align="right">covered up</td><td>otata 10</td></tr>
<tr><td align="right">faded prayer</td><td>A Hundred Gourds 4.4</td></tr>
<tr><td align="right">collecting flowers</td><td>Modern Haiku 47.2</td></tr>
<tr><td align="right">sooner in the bluer</td><td>The Heron's Nest XV:3</td></tr>
<tr><td align="right">the stars</td><td>otata 22</td></tr>
<tr><td align="right">a stone's throw</td><td>A Hundred Gourds 5.2</td></tr>
</table>

"silence" and "wind the sound" previously appeared in *Earth in Sunrise: International Haiku in Global Perspective* (Red Moon Press, 2017); "collecting flowers" also appeared in *They Gave us Life: Celebrating Mothers, Fathers, & Others in Haiku* (Middle Island Press, 2017); "sooner in the bluer" also appeared in *The Wonder Code* (Girasole Press, 2017).

culling into my dreams morning birds

silence   the heart   the heart   the heart

wind the sound of all else

all of the senses open sea

god the aperture wide

the call to prayer being air

a bird note
quotient of
the blue

it's enough if
at thought's edge
a crow

the poplar's way the storm moves

covered up
by fig leaves
the fall

faded prayer flags the color of wind

collecting flowers for mother a field

sooner in the bluer violets dusk

the stars blown into magnolias

a stone's throw shimmering moon

Debbi Antebi

Joseph Salvatore Aversano

Paul Chambers

Terri L French

Joshua Gage

Brent Goodman

Tia Haynes

Jessica Latham

Anna Maris

Elliot Nicely

Jacquie Pearce

Sandi Pray

Sharon Pretti

Dave Read

Hansha Teki

Angela Terry

Lew Watts

Paul Chambers

English Tutor

Born 7 March 1986
Newport Wales
Currently resides
Newport Wales

The hallmarks of Chambers' haiku are acute observation coupled with a great deal of natural empathy. We have long admired this approach, and, indeed, perhaps the most popular of all haiku poets, Issa, championed exactly these qualities. At the same time, because they are the expected values and techniques of the genre, something more must be present for such work to stand out. We discover this something more where the poet allows the poetic material to involve him. This is not to say he writes from the authorial "I" — in fact he rather eschews this — but that he allows himself to be a character in the play he witnesses unfolding. The natural pathos that arises out of these encounters imbues the other poems of the selection with a great sympathy, and the reader enters the poet's realm aware of the interconnectedness of all the things we find herein.

Credits

headland mist *hedgerow 92*
long afternoon *Presence 60*
sun in the ribs *bottle rockets 30*
endless stars *Presence 55*
leaf drifts *Frogpond 41.1*
convalescence *Frogpond 41.1*
evening frost *Presence 60*
moonless night *bottle rockets 35*
quieter now *Frogpond 36.1*
flooded field *Presence 56*
suddenly winter *Blithe Spirit 28.1*
the distance *hedgerow 85*
goshawk's cry *Modern Haiku 49.3*
church cross *Blithe Spirit 26.1*
freeing itself *hedgerow 85*

"convalescence" won the Museum of Haiku Literature Award for *Frogpond* 41.1.

headland mist
a curlew at the tip
of a cry

sun in the ribs
of the old pier
ebb tide

long afternoon . . .
the sky trickling
from a tide pool

leaf drifts . . .
an empty strip
of painkillers

convalescence . . .
autumn revealing
the river

endless stars . . .
the braille on the box
of sleeping pills

moonless night
the weight of the corners
of my mother's mouth

evening frost . . .
a television flickers
in an empty room

suddenly winter—
a stray dog
gnawing a stone

flooded field—
a heron pulls deeper
into winter

quieter now
than before it came
first snow

goshawk's cry
deep under snow
the road turns

church cross—
a crow displaces
a crow

the distance
of the harrier's cry
withered moor

freeing itself
of itself
the thawing stream

Debbi Antebi

Joseph Salvatore Aversano

Paul Chambers

Terri L French

Joshua Gage

Brent Goodman

Tia Haynes

Jessica Latham

Anna Maris

Elliot Nicely

Jacquie Pearce

Sandi Pray

Sharon Pretti

Dave Read

Hansha Teki

Angela Terry

Lew Watts

Terri L. French

Retired Massage Therapist

Born 16 September 1959
Pontiac MI
Currently resides
Huntsville AL

French's poems meet us at the front door, throw it wide open and invite us in. Their specificity ("owl pellets", "a full-spectrum lamp", "a folded napkin") authenticates the haiku moment for the reader. This is a poet who has a strong sense of self. French acknowledges the inevitability of aging, the complexity of relationships and her own fallibility with irony and humor. Within these poems we get a sense of shifting and reassembling until a balance can be found. In a straightforward, no-nonsense manner, French shows us what is, as she sees it, and allows us to make of it what we will. It is not difficult to find bits of one's own lived-in surroundings in such work, and her freshness and relatability make the reader feel right at home.

Credits

he brings flowers — *Frogpond 34:3*
gardenia blossoms — *A Hundred Gourds 1:4*
knit one purl two — previously unpublished
cowbird's song — *A Hundred Gourds 1:4*
autumn morning — *HNA Haiku Contest*
starry night — *Sketchbook July/August, 2011*
Ash Wednesday — *Modern Haiku 45:1*
winter gray — *failed haiku 2:15*
lingering fog — *Sonic Boom 3*
hangover — *failed haiku 1:2*
Easter morning — *Sonic Boom Senryu Contest*
autumn winds — *Daily Haiku February 15, 2011*
reconstructing — *The Heron's Nest XIII: 2*
winter solstice — *Under the Basho 2014*
spring thaw — *Under the Basho Contest*

"autumn morning" received an Honorable Mention in the Haiku North America Haiku Contest (2013); "starry night" took 1st Place for the July/August 2011 issue of *Sketchbook*; "Easter morning" took First Place in the 3rd Annual Senryu Contest (2017) organized by *Sonic Boom*; "spring thaw" took an Honorable Mention in the Under the Basho Haiku Contest in 2014.

he brings flowers
the same shade —
bruises

gardenia blossoms
at the border
of a repressed memory

knit one purl two
grandma lets
the secret slip

cowbird's song
an adopted child
brought home

autumn morning
the shape of a grandchild
beneath the quilt

starry night
we make up our own
constellations

Ash Wednesday
a whole congregation
with the same thumb print

winter gray
a full-spectrum lamp
for my half-assed mood

lingering fog
a pair of reading glasses
in every room

hangover
a mosquito comes back
for hair of the dog

Easter morning —
and I can't even
get out of bed

autumn winds
campaign signs
shifting positions

reconstructing
a field mouse —
owl pellets

winter solstice—
a folded napkin
beneath the table leg

spring thaw
an ice shanty leans
into the melt

Debbi Antebi

Joseph Salvatore Aversano

Paul Chambers

Terri L French

Joshua Gage

Brent Goodman

Tia Haynes

Jessica Latham

Anna Maris

Elliot Nicely

Jacquie Pearce

Sandi Pray

Sharon Pretti

Dave Read

Hansha Teki

Angela Terry

Lew Watts

Joshua Gage

College Instructor

Born 9 May 1980
Middleburg Heights OH
Currently resides
Cleveland OH

Writing is one way of moving through emotional devastation. The hard work of finding words to express our pain may help us to come to understand it better. Gage goes one step further and uses one art form (poetry) to suggest the healing power of another (jazz). There is something about jazz that draws us out of ourselves and gives us to the beat, where what is inexpressible may find consolation. Maybe it's the syncopation — just a touch out of step — that's relatable. Or perhaps it's the improvisation that offers encouragement for our own making-it-up-as-we-go-along efforts. The very nature of jazz speaks to unpredictability. Gage's poems move us from solitary listening to public presentation, a return to community that adds another step to the healing process. For a moment there is a connection with something besides the pain — an understanding and a nudge forward.

Credits

cicada husk — *Modern Haiku 48.1*
sunflower — *Incense Dreams 2.2*
hysterectomy scars — *Mayfly 61*
first snow — *Shamrock February 2017*
scratchy 78 — *hedgerow 107*
a sax solo — *hedgerow 107*
muted trumpet — *hedgerow 107*
whiskey tumbler — *hedgerow 110*
a dry Manhattan — *Haiku Canada Review October 2017*
spring moon — *bottle rockets 39*
satin dress — *hedgerow 107*
downtown commute — *World Haiku Review March 2018*
Amtrack — *bottle rockets 30*
abandoned factory — *bottle rockets 34*
autumn twilight — *The Heron's Nest XVIII.2*

cicada husk
the mark from my wedding ring
already fading

sunflower
the chickadee
shifts its grip

hysterectomy scars
the veined buds
of the orchid

first snow
the secrets my daughter
tells my wife

scratchy 78
the A-train syncopates
past my apartment

a sax solo
from the corner
the lightness of my bus fair

muted trumpet
a magnolia sunset
in the low stage lights

whiskey tumbler
full
of minor chord changes

a dry Manhattan
another night
spent in Tunisia

spring moon
his trumpet's slurred notes
against the train's backbeat

satin dress
the way her voice blues
the melody

downtown commute
through snow flurries
the soft glow of brake lights

Amtrack
the rituals
of strangers

abandoned factory—
seagulls gather
on the frozen river

autumn twilight—
the last pill
sticks to my tongue

Debbi Antebi

Joseph Salvatore Aversano

Paul Chambers

Terri L French

Joshua Gage

Brent Goodman

Tia Haynes

Jessica Latham

Anna Maris

Elliot Nicely

Jacquie Pearce

Sandi Pray

Sharon Pretti

Dave Read

Hansha Teki

Angela Terry

Lew Watts

Brent Goodman

Editor / Musician

Born 25 July 1971
Milwaukee WI
Currently resides
Rhinelander WI

The surest antidote to a romantic cast of mind is loss. Once we become aware of the abyss, our lives are forever marked, and we can't unknow the knowing. But loss is the not the ultimate decider of how we conduct our lives thereafter, but merely an inevitable part of the process of life. Whether or not we can retain our feel for redemption is what is truly endangered, and what we most ask our art to maintain. Goodman's haiku evince this romantic cast of mind — so many firsts, and so much belief — and evidence his personal sense of loss, especially in familial terms. But he doesn't lose hope, and it is the hope in the poems that make them appeal to us even as they comfort him. Such hope is ultimately personal, but at the point where articulation of grander truths is no longer possible, it is the personal that remains, as these poems attest.

Credits

<table>
<tr><td>milkweed pod</td><td>Frogpond 38.1</td></tr>
<tr><td>learning to weave</td><td>The Heron's Nest XVII:2</td></tr>
<tr><td>first house</td><td>bottle rockets 34</td></tr>
<tr><td>across the river</td><td>The Heron's Nest XV:4</td></tr>
<tr><td>vietnam</td><td>Modern Haiku 46.1</td></tr>
<tr><td>horseradish cheddar</td><td>failed haiku 4</td></tr>
<tr><td>Father's Day</td><td>A Hundred Gourds 5.1</td></tr>
<tr><td>spider</td><td>Modern Haiku 46.3</td></tr>
<tr><td>unable to articulate</td><td>Moongarlic 4</td></tr>
<tr><td>the flashing stone</td><td>17th Mainichi Haiku Contest</td></tr>
<tr><td>misreading the line</td><td>A Hundred Gourds 4.3</td></tr>
<tr><td>green corn moon</td><td>A Hundred Gourds 3.3</td></tr>
<tr><td>my body turns</td><td>Modern Haiku 46.2</td></tr>
<tr><td>singing a while</td><td>Take-Out Window</td></tr>
<tr><td>walking across</td><td>A Hundred Gourds 5.1</td></tr>
</table>

"spider" previously appeared in *dust devils: The Red Moon Anthology of English-Language Haiku 2016* (Red Moon Press, 2017); "the flashing stone" received an Honorable Mention in the 17th Mainichi Haiku Contest; "green corn moon" also appeared in *big data: The Red Moon Anthology of English-Language Haiku 2014* (Red Moon Press, 2015); "my body turns" also appeared in *Haiku 2016: 100 notable ku from 2015* (Modern Haiku Press, 2016).

milkweed pod even if we fell in love

learning to weave
one breath between us
the long night

first house
we carry our reflection
up the stairs

across the river
the other side
of my family

vietnam my father's given name

horseradish cheddar
sweet white grapes
after his funeral

Father's Day
I cast a spinner bait
into a tree

spider
unfolding with the lawn chair—
family reunion

unable to articulate any further the ocean

the flashing stone
out of water
fades into my hand

misreading the line where consciousness begins

green corn moon
finding the way home again
through my childhood

my body turns the milky way back into water

singing a while
without realizing it . . .
the Pleiades

walking across
the white river
Easter morning

Debbi Antebi

Joseph Salvatore Aversano

Paul Chambers

Terri L French

Joshua Gage

Brent Goodman

Tia Haynes

Jessica Latham

Anna Maris

Elliot Nicely

Jacquie Pearce

Sandi Pray

Sharon Pretti

Dave Read

Hansha Teki

Angela Terry

Lew Watts

Tia Haynes

Stay-at-Home Mom

Born 19 June 1985
Dayton OH
Currently resides
Lakewood OH

Haynes seems to open the pages of her journal and place them trustingly in the reader's hands. There is no putting on airs, no trying to be someone she is not. Instead, quietly and humbly the reader is shown where the poet has been and where she is now. It is not by any means a life free of struggle, but rather one from which she strives to heal ("therapy session", "support group"). Unsurprisingly, it is those closest to us who can hurt us the most. Haynes explores the many facets of family with the range of emotions that loaded topic can evoke. From the shadow cast by "family secrets" to the birth of a child ("late night bottle") to the release of another member ("mother's passing"), Haynes' light touch offers up these emotionally-charged life events without sentimentality. Seemingly effortless in their simplicity, these poems cohere in a voice newly discovered by the poet but in fact present all along.

Credits

family secrets	*Sonic Boom Senryu Contest 2017*
dandelions	previously unpublished
morning hike	*chrysanthemum 22*
cliff's edge	*chrysanthemum 22*
support group	*failed haiku 2:20*
the clocks	*failed haiku 2:24*
a doe	*cattails october 2018*
the earth's curve	*cattails april 2018*
late night bottle	*Blithe Spirit 28:1*
stretch marks	*#FemkuMag 2*
morning cartoons	*#FemkuMag 1*
dusk	*Golden Haiku Competition 2018*
memorial service	*failed haiku 2:19*
after packing	*Robert Spiess Haiku Award 2018*
mother's passing	*Incense Dreams 2:2*

"family secrets" took Third Prize in the *Sonic Boom* Senryu Contest 2017; "support group" appeared on *Haiku Commentary* on March 10, 2018; "late night bottle" also appeared in *Four Hundred and Two Snails: The Haiku Society of America Members' Anthology* (Haiku Society of America, 2018); "morning cartoons" also appeared in *a hole in the light: The Red Moon Anthology of English-Language Haiku 2018* (Red Moon Press, 2019); "dusk" received an Honorable Mention in the Golden Haiku Competition 2018; "after packing" was awarded First Prize in the Robert Spiess Memorial Haiku Award Competition 2018.

family secrets
a fly chooses
the butter

dandelions
all the little white lies
between us

morning hike
an unexpected turn
in our conversation

cliff's edge—
the fence post
leans in

support group
I never know
where to put my hands

the clocks
out of sync
therapy session

a doe
full with fawn
spring thaw

the earth's curve
entering the room
belly first

late night bottle
how our rocking
becomes a prayer

stretch marks
every road
that's led to you

morning cartoons
I shake out
the last pill

dusk
a discarded umbrella
gathers rain

memorial service
searching for meaning
in the carpet

after packing
our quiet
embrace

mother's passing
how I found
my voice

Debbi Antebi

Joseph Salvatore Aversano

Paul Chambers

Terri L French

Joshua Gage

Brent Goodman

Tia Haynes

Jessica Latham

Anna Maris

Elliot Nicely

Jacquie Pearce

Sandi Pray

Sharon Pretti

Dave Read

Hansha Teki

Angela Terry

Lew Watts

Jessica Latham

Inspirational Poet & Mother

Born 7 April 1982
San Diego CA
Currently resides
Valley Ford CA

These are joyful poems, poems that give full rein to the romantic element in all of us, that make us project our most confident, hopeful selves into the future, and that expect the best of the people and occurrences that await us there. Such work can be mocked as possessing too rosy an attitude, given our world and its inhabitants, but how much darker that world would be without poems that strive for the light. This is still the world where the scent of flowers — and love — may enthrall us, where we may daydream of the moments of grace that lie before our loved ones, where wishes may indeed have a chance of coming true. But residing only there would be a willful ignorance. What redeems these fancies is their being held, not in ignorance of how the world is, but in spite of it. It is indeed, ultimately, the lessons learned along the way that make this choosing cohere.

Credits

snow crocus	previously unpublished
jasmine breeze	*Stardust February 2018*
how openly	*Snapshot Calendar 2019*
french lavender	*tinywords 18.1*
feeling into	previously unpublished
ripening peaches	*Art of Haiku 2017*
dandelion fluff	*hedgerow 113*
leaf rustle	*hedgerow 121*
falling snow	*Cricket Song*
shoes on the wrong feet	*Wild Plum 3.2*
first day of school	*Frogpond 38.3*
our footprints	*Seasons of Haiku Trail*
a cicada	*Ephemerae 1:2*
drunk at noon	*tinywords 18.1*
river rain	*hedgerow 118*

"how openly" placed in the Snapshot Press Calendar Competition in 2019; "ripening peaches" was a semi-finalist in the Art of Haiku Grand Prix for May 2017; "dandelion fluff" also appeared in *all this bowing* (buddha baby press, 2017); "falling snow" first appeared in *Cricket Song: Haiku and Short Poems from a Mother's Heart* (Red Moon Press, 2017); "our footprints" is featured at the Seasons of Haiku Trail at the Holden Arboretum, Kirtland OH.

snow crocus
watching the way
you watch me

jasmine breeze
he inhales
my breath

how openly
it holds the rain . . .
magnolia blossom

french lavender . . .
in love with a song
I don't understand

feeling into the fall rose petals

ripening peaches
fall at the slightest touch . . .
first love

dandelion fluff
the silly things
I still wish for

leaf rustle uncovering my inner child

falling snow
how quietly you take root
in my womb

shoes on the wrong feet
someday he'll ask a girl
to dance

first day of school
tying the vines
to the trellis

our footprints
become a memory . . .
spring moon

a cicada
somewhere in the house
loneliness

drunk at noon
in my next life make me
a honeybee

river rain
these old lessons
again and again

Debbi Antebi

Joseph Salvatore Aversano

Paul Chambers

Terri L French

Joshua Gage

Brent Goodman

Tia Haynes

Jessica Latham

Anna Maris

Elliot Nicely

Jacquie Pearce

Sandi Pray

Sharon Pretti

Dave Read

Hansha Teki

Angela Terry

Lew Watts

Anna Maris

Journalist

Born 12 April 1970
Malmö Sweden
Currently resides
Hässleholm Sweden

Maris's is a distinctive voice — modern, literate, moody and often dark. It breathes a patience, undoubtedly brought on by geographical exigencies, as well as an earned knowing of self. How deftly she turns a line from Dickinson to her, and haiku's, purpose ("shallow breathing"). How quietly she locates the truth, whether suggested by others ("low autumn sun") or discovered by herself ("bus stop"). There are reasons for concern ("gathering clouds") or perhaps even despair ("drowning slowly"). But the omens of revival are not lost upon her, whatever the consequences of such things may be ("spring rain"). The question, ultimately, is whether these things are enough. We join her when, in a moment of exultation ("above all") she finds a surfeit of joy.

Credits

spring rain	*Sharpening the Green Pencil Contest*
a room	previously unpublished
shallow breathing	*Lifedeathetc*
summer holiday	*The New English Verse*
drowning slowly	*Under the Basho 2018*
midnight sun	*#FemkuMag 8*
orion's belt	*Atlas Poetica 25*
saturday lie-in	*failed haiku 11*
bus stop	*Frogpond 36:3*
gathering clouds	*Lifedeathetc*
low autumn sun	*#FemkuMag 5*
scarlet leaves	*hedgerow 100*
wondering what	*#FemkuMag 7*
just when i thought	*hedgerow 125*
above all	*Under the Basho 2017*

"spring rain" was Commended in the 2016 Sharpening the Green Pencil Haiku Contest; "shallow breathing" and "gathering clouds" first appeared in *Lifedeathetc* (Red Moon Press, 2016); "summer holiday" previously appeared in *The New English Verse* (Cyberwit, 2017); "bus stop" also appeared in *fear of dancing: The Red Moon Press Anthology of English-Language Haiku 2013* (Red Moon Press, 2014).

spring rain
an old letter
unfolded again

a room
between leather bound backs
of my own

shallow breathing that thing with feathers

summer holiday
the almost endless stretch
of white beach

drowning slowly the sound as we walk

midnight sun
our wedding night over
in minutes

orion's belt
watching the same stars
our ancestors

saturday lie-in
again i miss the train
in my dream

bus stop
the old man
never gets on

gathering clouds
the sea claims the sand
under my feet

low autumn sun
again you call me
your last love

scarlet leaves
a black umbrella turns
inside out

wondering what he sees in her tulips

just when i thought
it was too late
tadpoles

above all skylark

Debbi Antebi

Joseph Salvatore Aversano

Paul Chambers

Terri L French

Joshua Gage

Brent Goodman

Tia Haynes

Jessica Latham

Anna Maris

Elliot Nicely

Jacquie Pearce

Sandi Pray

Sharon Pretti

Dave Read

Hansha Teki

Angela Terry

Lew Watts

Elliot Nicely

Teacher

Born 4 July 1976
Sandusky OH
Currently resides
Lakewood OH

The particulars point to the not-quite-right — phrases such as "flowering bittersweet", "false spring", "droop of sunflowers". These poems have a sense of striving as the poet attempts to make up the difference. It makes sense, of course, for a poet to approach rectification through words. We witness Nicely searching for the right words for an argument, a confession, an apology, and a small funeral. With one for whom words are so important, "that which is unsaid" becomes all the more profound. Even then there are instances "where words fail." Employing an objective, unsentimental style, these poems on the less-than-what-could-be give an impression of the poet's stoic perseverance. They seem to say, "I'm doing the best I can. I'm still trying." And surely the "chances I did take" count for something.

Credits

flowering bittersweet *Acorn 38*
indian summer *bottle rockets 25*
that which is unsaid *Moonset 6.1*
storm waves *bottle rockets 28*
her eyes *Modern Haiku 43.1*
where words fail *Kokako 22*
first day of school *Modern Haiku 44.1*
autumn migration *Frogpond 40.2*
shoebox burial *Modern Haiku 40.2*
halloween *Presence 58*
dentist office window *Frogpond 36.1*
browning lilacs *Presence 56*
waiting *Frogpond 33.2*
winter constellations *Acorn 37*
cloud shadows *Modern Haiku 48.2*

"where words fail" also appeared in *galaxy of dust: The Red Moon Anthology of English-Language Haiku 2015* (Red Moon Press, 2016) and *Butterfly Dream: 66 Selected English-Chinese Bilingual Haiku IV* (NeverEnding Story, 2018); "halloween" also appeared in *old song: The Red Moon Anthology of English-Language Haiku 2017* (Red Moon Press, 2018); "dentist office window" and "winter constellations" were awarded Lit Youngstown's 2017 Words Made Visible Prize; "waiting" also appeared in *evolution: The Red Moon Anthology of English-Language Haiku 2010* (Red Moon Press, 2011) and *Like the Pumpkins* (The Befuddled Press, 2015); "cloud shadows" also appeared in *They Gave Us Life: Celebrating Mothers, Fathers & Others in Haiku* (Middle Island Press, 2017).

flowering bittersweet . . .
the chances
i did take

indian summer
. . . the rest of
our argument

that which is unsaid
—condensation
streaks the window

storm waves
through the winter wheat
how wrong I've been

her eyes
avoid my apology
false spring

where words fail pines along the cliff's edge

first day of school the droop of sunflowers

autumn migration
the pull of my son's hand
from mine

shoebox burial
the deceased
in prada

halloween:
death takes two
pieces of candy

dentist office window:
the jack-o'-lantern's
toothless grin

browning lilacs
the months since
my last confession

waiting
for her lab results
the black between stars

winter constellations
all these roads again
leading home

cloud shadows . . .
I remember for
both of us

Debbi Antebi

Joseph Salvatore Aversano

Paul Chambers

Terri L French

Joshua Gage

Brent Goodman

Tia Haynes

Jessica Latham

Anna Maris

Elliot Nicely

Jacquie Pearce

Sandi Pray

Sharon Pretti

Dave Read

Hansha Teki

Angela Terry

Lew Watts

Jacquie Pearce

Writer

Born 27 January 1962
Vancouver BC Canada
Currently resides
Burnaby BC Canada

It is the linear effect — the shortest distance between two points — that seems most of interest to this poet; how we are directed and moved from place to place. A bus route, a roller coaster track, dog barks that "domino" down a street, a line outside an emergency shelter, a viaduct, even the progression of a dream. Trains in particular figure prominently. That a train has a predestined route seems of importance. In Pearce's work, this straight line seems to lead from childhood innocence ("happy face") where we delight in simple pleasures such as the "whistle in a blade of grass," enjoying a fudgsicle, and drawing in condensation on a bus window, to the harshness of an urban environment with its homelessness, abuse and "gunfire at night." At the end of the line the poet still can dream — one with jagged edges, but a dream nonetheless.

Credits

morning bus — previously unpublished
rollercoaster — previously unpublished
summer walk — previously unpublished
sunlit afternoon — *The Heron's Nest XX.3*
warm prairie breeze — previously unpublished
evening train whistle — *The Heron's Nest XIV.4*
wind-stirred night — *DailyHaiku Cycle 8*
sparrows shelter — *DailyHaiku Cycle 8*
fog-shrouded windows — *DailyHaiku Cycle 8*
snowfall — previously unpublished
temperature drop — previously unpublished
spare change — previously unpublished
biting wind — previously unpublished
under the viaduct — previously unpublished
gunfire at night — previously unpublished

"sunlit afternoon" also appeared in *a hole in the light: The Red Moon Anthology of English-Language Haiku 2018* (Red Moon Press, 2019); "sparrows shelter" also appeared in *A History of Haiku in Canada* by Terry Ann Carter (Brick Books, 2015).

morning bus
a happy face
in the window fog

rollercoaster
a small boy eyes
the minimum height bar

summer walk
the length of
a fudgesicle

sunlit afternoon
finding the whistle
in a blade of grass

warm prairie breeze
the porter plays harmonica
in the open door

evening train whistle—
my grandfather's habit
of checking his watch

wind-stirred night
dog barks domino
down the street

sparrows shelter
under the 7-11 sign
October wind

fog-shrouded windows—
the train commuters
turn inward

snowfall . . .
the muffled clank
of shunting rail cars

temperature drop
the long line outside
the emergency shelter

spare change
she gives me the story
of her bruise

biting wind
tearing up another
lottery ticket

under the viaduct
the homeless man
sits zazen

gunfire at night
the jagged edges
of my dreams

Debbi Antebi

Joseph Salvatore Aversano

Paul Chambers

Terri L French

Joshua Gage

Brent Goodman

Tia Haynes

Jessica Latham

Anna Maris

Elliot Nicely

Jacquie Pearce

Sandi Pray

Sharon Pretti

Dave Read

Hansha Teki

Angela Terry

Lew Watts

Sandi Pray

Retired Media Specialist

Born 16 June 1949
Olney MD
Currently resides
St Johns FL

An artist often is influenced by her surroundings — for Pray, this means the prairie. The connection she feels disports itself through her predilection for bird images: migrating cranes, herons, blue feathers and crows. Birds are her company, confidantes and advisors. Not only the lifting of the wind but also the sounds that accompany it are of note: birdsong, the "sound of wind" finding empty places, a tone as bold as a banjo and as light as "the clicking of dragonfly wings." Of course what is seen and unseen is also of interest. The poet notices "a stone too lovely to skip" and demonstrates visual and mental focus in a sumi-e lesson until all the "world has become a bamboo shoot." Equal emphasis is given to negative space: "the sound of no one," silence, and what "the sky unsays." Pray's poems paint the sights and sounds of prairie life with practiced brushstrokes.

Credits

<table>
<tr><td align="right">a lifetime</td><td>previously unpublished</td></tr>
<tr><td align="right">migrating cranes</td><td>The Heron's Nest XIX.4</td></tr>
<tr><td align="right">wingbeats</td><td>Indian Kukai</td></tr>
<tr><td align="right">blue feathers</td><td>Modern Haiku 49.2</td></tr>
<tr><td align="right">with an answer</td><td>Wild Plum Haiku Contest</td></tr>
<tr><td align="right">frog song</td><td>previously unpublished</td></tr>
<tr><td align="right">empty places</td><td>previously unpublished</td></tr>
<tr><td align="right">raindrops</td><td>previously unpublished</td></tr>
<tr><td align="right">evening jam</td><td>Akitsu Spring 18</td></tr>
<tr><td align="right">sumi-e lesson</td><td>previously unpublished</td></tr>
<tr><td align="right">river walk</td><td>previously unpublished</td></tr>
<tr><td align="right">august heat</td><td>A Heron's Nest XIX.2</td></tr>
<tr><td align="right">only the clicking</td><td>previously unpublished</td></tr>
<tr><td align="right">slow afternoon</td><td>previously unpublished</td></tr>
<tr><td align="right">autumn twilight</td><td>previously unpublished</td></tr>
</table>

"wingbeats" placed 5th in the Indian Kukai #24 in 2017; "with an answer" was awarded First Prize in the Wild Plum Haiku Contest 2017.

a lifetime
of grass in my hair
prairie wind

migrating cranes
until mountains
come between us

wingbeats
sometimes just knowing
i'm not alone

blue feathers
all but the song
in my hand

with an answer
for everything
the tree of crows

frog song
a heron's shadow
takes the last note

empty places
the sound of wind
finding them

raindrops
the first few notes
of an old song

evening jam
a banjo picks
through the wind

sumi-e lesson
my world has become
a bamboo shoot

river walk
in my hand the stone
too lovely to skip

august heat
the sound of no one
behind me

only the clicking
of dragonfly wings
hospital garden

slow afternoon
a clerk wipes nothing
from the window

autumn twilight
the sky unsays
everything

Debbi Antebi

Joseph Salvatore Aversano

Paul Chambers

Terri L French

Joshua Gage

Brent Goodman

Tia Haynes

Jessica Latham

Anna Maris

Elliot Nicely

Jacquie Pearce

Sandi Pray

Sharon Pretti

Dave Read

Hansha Teki

Angela Terry

Lew Watts

Sharon Pretti

Medical Social Worker

Born 23 May 1962
San Francisco CA
Currently resides
San Francisco CA

The Japanese aesthetic of *yūgen* suggests that which is beyond what can be seen; mystery. It is an invitation to move into a poem to look around the river's bend to see what might lie ahead. Our curiosity draws us in. Too much *yūgen* and a reader may become lost in fog walking in circles looking for a way out. Pretti strikes just the right balance, drawing our attention to what is not visible in order to emphasize what is or what could be. She favors words and phrases — "unspoken," "unexplored," "her absence," "the call never made" — as examples of this mysterious element. Sometimes there is a hint of a moment just before we came on the scene: "the hours after visiting hours," "the names erased." The poet doesn't offer answers but rather raises questions that lead to further questions as we ponder the idea that we too move on, leaving behind absences of our own.

Credits

redwood grove — previously unpublished
prognosis — *Wild Plum Fall/Winter 2017*
wake of a mallard — *A Splash of Water*
river stones — *Wild Plum Spring/Summer 2017*
moon sliver — *Mariposa 37*
the hills after rain — *Acorn 39*
pointing out — *Acorn 35*
test results pending — *Full of Moonlight*
hint of rain — *Frogpond 39.3*
mist off the river — *Mariposa 33*
the names erased — *Modern Haiku 47.2*
speaking to him — *Acorn 36*
lonelier — *Acorn 32*
somewhere else — *Mariposa 34*
monarch migration — *on down the road*

"wake of a mallard' first appeared in *A Splash of Water* (HSA Members' Anthology, 2015); "test results pending" first appeared in *Full of Moonlight* (HSA Members' Anthology, 2016); "hint of rain" also appeared in *old song: The Red Moon Anthology of English-Language Haiku 2017* (Red Moon Press, 2018), Wishbone Moon (Jacar Press, 2018), and *Open Iris* (Two Autumns Press, 2018); "lonelier" was a Winner of The Haiku Calendar Competition 2017 and appeared in *The Haiku Calendar 2018* (Snapshot Press, 2018); "somewhere else" received an Honorable Mention in the 2015 San Francisco International Haiku Competition; "monarch migration" first appeared in *on down the road* (HSA Members' Anthology, 2017).

redwood grove . . .
the parts of my life
I leave unspoken

prognosis—
the shells he collects
between tides

wake of a mallard
each exhalation
a little longer

river stones
what's still unexplored
between us

moon sliver
the pin that holds
her bone in place

the hills after rain
I try to imagine
her absence

pointing out
which keepsakes will be mine
Mother's Day

text results pending the sway of palms

hint of rain
the hours after
visiting hours

mist off the river
the long distance call
never made

the names erased
from my address book
water's edge

speaking to him
as if he's still here
sea stars

lonelier
than I thought I was
wintering gulls

somewhere else
the right words spoken
sea fog

monarch migration
it begins again
my life story

Debbi Antebi

Joseph Salvatore Aversano

Paul Chambers

Terri L French

Joshua Gage

Brent Goodman

Tia Haynes

Jessica Latham

Anna Maris

Elliot Nicely

Jacquie Pearce

Sandi Pray

Sharon Pretti

Dave Read

Hansha Teki

Angela Terry

Lew Watts

Dave Read

Gas & Power Manager

Born 2 July 1970
Edmonton AB Canada
Currently resides
Calgary AB Canada

Every poem, every utterance, is a map, a key to navigating the hinterland, or skirting a coast. Ergo a poet is a mapmaker. But while we supply these hints about the known, the testable, in truth it is what there is to be discovered "off the map" that defies and most intrigues us. There are no ready phrases to express these states — it's all up to us to communicate what we find there, if it is communicable at all. Read sends us clues of his travels, but they keep returning to the known — the image of a bear where fear might dress itself differently; fog obscuring a clearer look at what's ahead. And he manages humor and pathos along the way. But the image that won't cohere — that which lurks in our ancient DNA — is what challenges us most, and which we can't evade, even if our prayers turn to smoke, and we let our most intimate communications go to voicemail.

Credits

all that shines *Presence 59*
wilderness trail *Frogpond 38.3*
mountain trail *tinywords 17.2*
not looking *failed haiku 2.5*
fading light *Presence 57*
more bruise *Wild Plum 3.2*
darkness *Acorn 37*
just another phase *Bones 14*
night frost *Haiku Canada Review 11.2*
October rain *bottle rockets 34*
evening train *Otata 16*
spare change *bottle rockets 35*
candle smoke *Modern Haiku 47.3*
twilight *Under The Basho 2016*
night winds *Frogpond 39.1*

"fading light" also appeared in *old song: The Red Moon Anthology of English Language Haiku 2017* (Red Moon Press, 2018); "darkness" received a Touchstone Award for Individual Poems from The Haiku Foundation in 2016.

all that shines
in a magpie's nest . . .
morning frost

wilderness trail
he wanders off the edge
of his map

mountain trail . . .
a bear crosses
his mind

not looking
ahead too far
autumn fog

fading light
her child's name
fills the street

more bruise
than banana
autumn deepens

darkness . . .
her name slips
into it

just another phase of the moonlight child

night frost
her reptilian
DNA

October rain
Captain America
shields his candy

evening train
I squeeze into
my headphones

spare change
my conscience empties
my pockets

candle smoke
the afterlife
of prayer

twilight
every bird
a crow

night winds
I let her go
to voicemail

Debbi Antebi

Joseph Salvatore Aversano

Paul Chambers

Terri L French

Joshua Gage

Brent Goodman

Tia Haynes

Jessica Latham

Anna Maris

Elliot Nicely

Jacquie Pearce

Sandi Pray

Sharon Pretti

Dave Read

Hansha Teki

Angela Terry

Lew Watts

Hansha Teki

Retired

Born 17 September 1949
Paparoa New Zealand
Currently resides
Paraparaumu New Zealand

We can't look at this work as we do most haiku. The poet clearly is trying to expand the genre. Does he succeed? If success is measured in creating interest in the reader, then the answer is an overwhelming "yes." There are few unmistakeable voices in haiku, but on the basis of this sampling, Teki's is one. The poet seeks nothing less than an active engagement with the protean present, using the tools of a poet — that is, through words. These poems seem uncertain if words are a useful tool for such a quest, but what else is there? If we are left with their "emptied skins," at least they supply us their echoes and dreams, and we can arrange it so that their "white spaces / fit together." We follow the white spaces when traversing a maze, so perhaps this is the most we can hope for. It is an extra solace, perhaps, if in the end this also leads us to "the beginnings / of touch."

Credits

last rites	*The Heron's Nest XIV:3*
twilight mist	*Haibun Today 11.4*
empty room	*failed haiku 14*
nightfall	*Autumn Moon Haiku Journal 1.1*
a dream	*Otata 3*
emptied	*Bones 14*
autumn dusk	*Simply Haiku 10.1*
a word for	previously unpublished
post-literate verse	previously unpublished
turbulent mist	*naad anunaad*
river fog	*Frogpond 35.3*
in becoming	previously unpublished
a word	*Bones 8*
moonless	previously unpublished
by late night	previously unpublished

"turbulent mist" first appeared in *naad anunaad — an anthology of contemporary world haiku* (Vishwakarma Publications, 2016); "a word" also appeared in *Haiku 2016* (Modern Haiku Press, 2017) and *Poetry as Consciousness* (Keibunsha Company Ltd., 2018).

last rites—
I watch her eyes
let go of me

twilight mist
whisper-words
hang about

empty room—
I enter the sound
of my echo

nightfall—
an absence of stars
closes in

a dream I make of the just now

emptied
of itself
the skin of words

autumn dusk . . .
the descent of light
into its past

a word for hope hollowed of vowels

post-literate verse
all the white spaces
fit together

turbulent mist—
all that is to become
lost in becoming

river fog—
a nameless ache
fills the page

in becoming a loss of snow

a word
after a word
at war
Afterwards

moonless nostalgia for the unknown

by late light
the beginnings
of touch

Debbi Antebi

Joseph Salvatore Aversano

Paul Chambers

Terri L French

Joshua Gage

Brent Goodman

Tia Haynes

Jessica Latham

Anna Maris

Elliot Nicely

Jacquie Pearce

Sandi Pray

Sharon Pretti

Dave Read

Hansha Teki

Angela Terry

Lew Watts

Angela Terry

Retired

Born 18 July 1948
Seattle WA
Currently resides
Lake Forest Park WA

Haiku is a poetry of nouns — specific, tangible things. For Terry, however, things not necessarily held in one's hand are as real and potent as those that are. What is the "half life of a memory" or the "weight of yes"? The "language of trees" or the "birth of wind"? The poet juxtaposes these non-things with the concrete. These poems ask the reader to draw from both sides of the brain — to slip a little out of our comfort zone. This discomfort begs the reader to engage and look for connections to span the gap. It is here that an aha moment may occur when we see the ordinary in a new way. Terry is consistently able to see what others don't, or else to see the same thing but askew ("how differently we see the sky"). Her poems walk readers to the ordinary, then tilt the paper just slightly so we can see what she sees — not something necessarily grasped, but something rather that needs to be taken in.

Credits

<table>
<tr><td>morning moon</td><td>ephemerae 1a</td></tr>
<tr><td>spring rain</td><td>Modern Haiku 49.1</td></tr>
<tr><td>lost in</td><td>Acorn 40</td></tr>
<tr><td>how differently</td><td>A Hundred Gourds 3:2</td></tr>
<tr><td>withholding</td><td>Modern Haiku 46.1</td></tr>
<tr><td>deep within</td><td>chrysanthemum 23</td></tr>
<tr><td>crescent moon</td><td>cattails October 2017</td></tr>
<tr><td>night train</td><td>Modern Haiku 49.2</td></tr>
<tr><td>the labyrinth walk</td><td>Acorn 41</td></tr>
<tr><td>maybe I need</td><td>Acorn 35</td></tr>
<tr><td>stripping off</td><td>Modern Haiku 49.2</td></tr>
<tr><td>wind chill</td><td>Modern Haiku 45.1</td></tr>
<tr><td>autumn butterfly</td><td>The Heron's Nest XIX.2</td></tr>
<tr><td>within its silence</td><td>chrysanthemum 20</td></tr>
<tr><td>a fragrant wind</td><td>Shiki Kukai June 2014</td></tr>
</table>

"night train" took First Honorable Mention in The Robert Spiess Memorial Haiku Award 2018; "a fragrant wind" won First Place in the kigo section of the Shiki Kukai for June 2014.

morning moon—
the half life
of memory

spring rain . . .
the weight of "yes"
between us

lost in
the morning mist
the language of trees

how differently
we see the sky
blue morpho

withholding
so much information
summer stars

deep within
a grove of redwoods
the birth of the wind

crescent moon
so many dreams
turned sideways

night train . . .
the false positive
that wasn't

the labyrinth walk
dotted with daisies . . .
he loved me once

maybe I need
a different compass . . .
windblown clouds

stripping off
the wallpaper
autumn rain

wind chill . . .
so much my parents
never talked of

autumn butterfly
the beauty
of last things

within its silence
all silence
snow moon

a fragrant wind . . .
the things we remember
when we're alone

Debbi Antebi

Joseph Salvatore Aversano

Paul Chambers

Terri L French

Joshua Gage

Brent Goodman

Tia Haynes

Jessica Latham

Anna Maris

Elliot Nicely

Jacquie Pearce

Sandi Pray

Sharon Pretti

Dave Read

Hansha Teki

Angela Terry

Lew Watts

Lew Watts

Retired to Writing

Born 15 February 1953
Cardiff Wales
Currently resides
Chicago IL

Watts has a feel for the precise and unusual word. It is unlikely we will be able to use "unbecoming" or "overpunctuate" again without feeling a debt. And it is through such precision that certain effects, such as irony, best present themselves. Here we will readily identify a slightly distanced persona coolly mooting the circumstances, be it the sharing of stories, the settling of ice in a glass, or the deepening of snow. But all of this is mere subterfuge — the real story of these poems — of all our poems — is pain. The poet displays a willingness to share his, especially that which has arisen out of disappointment: in relationships ("sickle moon", "wild juniper"), in the world ("home from war", "retirement day"), and, most keenly, with himself ("ice settles", "picking at threads"), without ever losing his faith in his fellow creatures, and hope ("slow descent").

Credits

slow descent	*Financial Times November 19, 2014*
home from war	*The Heron's Nest XVI.2*
his secret closet	*Bones 14*
sickle moon	*Modern Haiku 49.1*
Möbius strip	*A Hundred Gourds 4.4*
ice settles	*Modern Haiku 42.2*
eighteenth birthday	*bottle rockets 32*
his old lego set	*Modern Haiku 54.2*
old photograph	*Frogpond 36.2*
wild juniper	*bottle rockets 34*
picking at threads	*Frogpond 36.2*
retirement day	*Modern Haiku 45.2*
post-vasectomy	*Modern Haiku 48.2*
gone to her mother's	*Frogpond 40.2*
trial separation	*Frogpond 40.3*

"home from war" was nominated for a 2014 Touchstone Award, and also appeared in *big data: The Red Moon Anthology of English-Language Haiku 2014* (Red Moon Press, 2015); "post-vasectomy" also appeared in *Four Hundred and Two Snails: 2018 Haiku Society of America Members' Anthology* (HSA Members' Anthology, 2018); "trial separation" won an Honorable Mention in the 2017 Harold G. Henderson Haiku Contest (Haiku Society of America).

slow descent—
this sudden urge to share
life stories

home from war
we ease out
the champagne corks

his secret closet unbecoming a man

sickle moon
the old priest whispers
me too

Möbius strip
the topology
of tumble-dried bras

ice settles
in a morning scotch
things fall into place

eighteenth birthday—
our son graduates
to two syllables

his old lego set—
if I swallow
I'll choke

old photograph—
my son asks why my mother
married me

wild juniper
the way she was
after gin

picking at threads
of a worn seam—
still not forgiven

retirement day—
I move spam
to my inbox

post-vasectomy,
this 'primal' urge
to overpunctuate

gone to her mother's . . .
another lemon pit
misses the ashtray

trial separation
another inch of snow
on the gin bottles

Debbi Antebi

Joseph Salvatore Aversano

Paul Chambers

Terri L French

Joshua Gage

Brent Goodman

Tia Haynes

Jessica Latham

Anna Maris

Elliot Nicely

Jacquie Pearce

Sandi Pray

Sharon Pretti

Dave Read

Hansha Teki

Angela Terry

Lew Watts

Made in the USA
Monee, IL
07 July 2026

56544279R00111